THE
NBA
A HISTORY OF HOOPS

Published by Creative Education
P.O. Box 227, Mankato, Minnesota 56002
Creative Education is an imprint of The Creative Company
www.thecreativecompany.us

Design and production by Christine Vanderbeek
Art direction by Rita Marshall

Printed by Corporate Graphics in the United States of America

Photographs by Basketballphoto.com (Steve Lipofsky), Corbis (Underwood & Underwood), Dreamstime (Munktcu), Getty Images (Nathaniel S. Butler/NBAE, Gary Dineen/NBAE, Ned Dishman/NBAE, Barry Gossage/NBAE, Andy Hayt/NBAE, Jed Jacobsohn, Craig Jones, Jumper, Carol Kohen, Fernando Medina/NBAE, NBA Photo Library/NBAE, David Sherman/NBAE, SM/AIUEO, Ron Turenne/NBAE, Phil Walter), iStockphoto (Brandon Laufenberg), US Presswire

Library of Congress Cataloging-in-Publication Data
Nichols, John, 1966-
The story of the Toronto Raptors / by John Nichols.
p. cm. — (The NBA: a history of hoops)
Includes index.
Summary: The history of the Toronto Raptors professional basketball team from its start in 1995 to today, spotlighting the franchise's greatest players and reliving its most dramatic moments.
ISBN 978-1-58341-963-2
1. Toronto Raptors (Basketball team)—History—Juvenile literature.
2. Basketball—Ontario—Toronto—History—Juvenile literature. I. Title. II. Series.
GV885.52.T67N53 2010   796.323'64'0975924—dc22   2009036118

CPSIA: 120109 PO1093

First Edition
2 4 6 8 9 7 5 3 1

Page 3: The Raptor, Toronto's mascot
Pages 4–5: Guard DeMar DeRozan

THE STORY OF THE

TORONTO RAPTORS

JOHN NICHOLS

CREATIVE EDUCATION

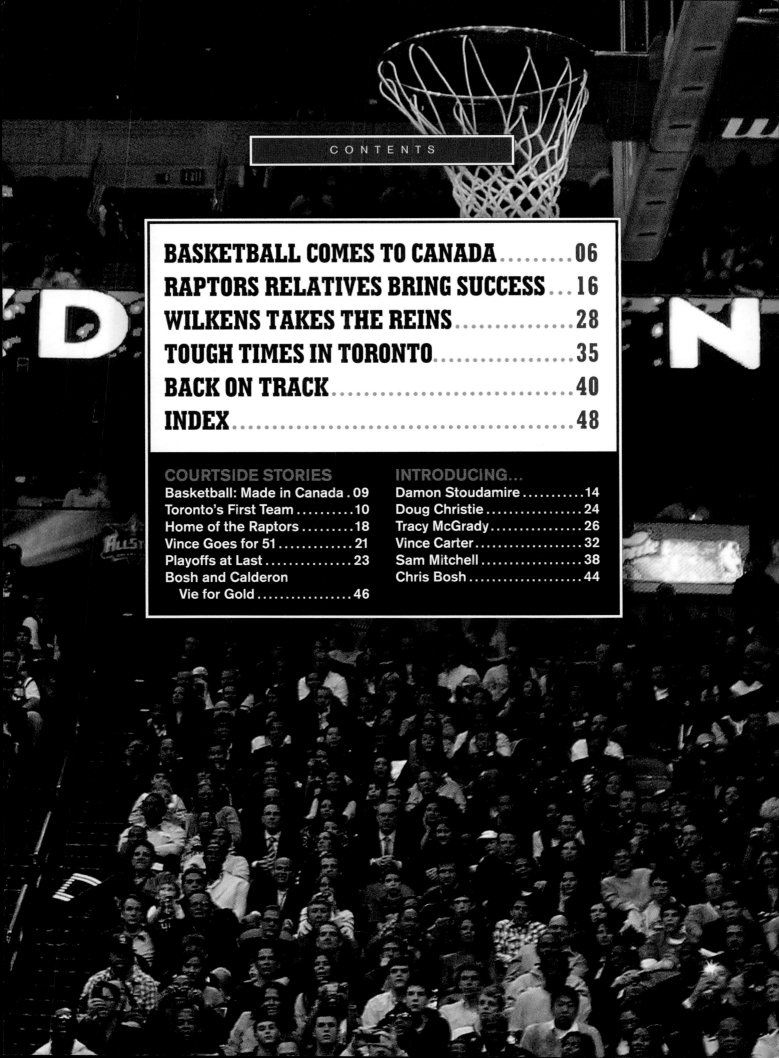

CONTENTS

BASKETBALL COMES TO CANADA 06
RAPTORS RELATIVES BRING SUCCESS ... 16
WILKENS TAKES THE REINS 28
TOUGH TIMES IN TORONTO 35
BACK ON TRACK 40
INDEX 48

COURTSIDE STORIES
Basketball: Made in Canada . 09
Toronto's First Team 10
Home of the Raptors 18
Vince Goes for 51 21
Playoffs at Last 23
Bosh and Calderon
   Vie for Gold 46

INTRODUCING...
Damon Stoudamire 14
Doug Christie 24
Tracy McGrady 26
Vince Carter 32
Sam Mitchell 38
Chris Bosh 44

CHAPTER ONE

BASKETBALL COMES TO CANADA

Located along the shores of Lake Ontario, Toronto is Canada's largest city. Toronto was founded in the late 1700s as a small British fort and has grown to become Ontario's provincial capital and one of the world's most diverse and vibrant cities. More than half of Toronto's nearly three million citizens were born outside of Canada, and many of them were attracted to the city's flourishing financial sector, telecommunications industry, and tradition of fine arts. Toronto also boasts one of the world's most recognizable skylines. The CN Tower, the world's second-tallest freestanding structure, rises majestically from the heart of the city, surrounded by a combination of historic buildings and modern skyscrapers that uniquely define Toronto's significant past and energetic present.

In tune with Toronto's diverse population, the city's sports scene also provides its citizens with a wide variety of choices. For many decades, its professional hockey team, the Toronto

Toronto is Canada's biggest city by far and the fifth-most populous in North America, home to more than two and a half million people.

Maple Leafs, dominated the hearts and minds of citizens. But in 1993, Toronto sports fans were given a new team to cheer for when the National Basketball Association (NBA) decided to expand into Canada and awarded the city a franchise. A public naming contest was held, and the winning entry was Raptors, in honor of a swift and deadly dinosaur—the velociraptor—that was made popular by the 1993 movie *Jurassic Park*.

When the NBA became interested in expanding to Canada during the early 1990s, businessman John Bitove Jr. led the effort to land a team for Toronto. Bitove had been a good amateur basketball player before establishing a successful investment firm, and he was convinced that the people of Toronto would support an NBA team. Although he was only in his early 30s, young for an NBA team owner, Bitove's enthusiastic campaign won over league officials. On November 4, 1993, the NBA officially announced that Toronto would become the league's 28th franchise, starting up play in the Eastern Conference's Central Division in 1995.

BASKETBALL: MADE IN CANADA

Dr. James Naismith offers instruction to two students of the game in 1926.

AROUND THE WORLD, MOST FANS OF BASKETBALL BELIEVE THE SPORT FINDS ITS ORIGINS IN THE UNITED STATES. While it's true that the game's founder, James Naismith, is credited with inventing basketball while living in Springfield, Massachusetts, in 1891, what most people do not know is that Naismith was Canadian. Born in a small township near Almonte, Ontario, Naismith grew up to be a fine athlete, playing football and soccer and performing in gymnastics in college. After graduating from Montreal's McGill University, he moved to the U.S. to take a job as a physical education teacher at a YMCA in Springfield. Asked by his boss to invent an indoor game to "provide an athletic distraction" for his unruly students, Naismith came up with the sport he called Basket Ball. The original game featured 13 basic rules and bore only a passing resemblance to today's sport, but Naismith's students grew to love it, and the game's popularity expanded quickly. More than a century later, millions around the world enjoy the graceful, athletic game of basketball, and it's all thanks to one of Canada's favorite sons.

MOST PEOPLE BELIEVE THE HISTORY OF PROFESSIONAL BASKETBALL IN CANADA BEGAN WHEN THE TORONTO RAPTORS AND VANCOUVER GRIZZLIES BEGAN LEAGUE PLAY IN 1995. But the truth is, Toronto's NBA roots reach all the way back to 1946. That year, the Basketball Association of America (BAA) was founded, with the Toronto Huskies as 1 of its 11 original teams. The first game in BAA history featured the Huskies playing host to the New York Knickerbockers on November 1, 1946, before a crowd of 7,090 fans at Toronto's Maple Leaf Gardens. Toronto lost that first game and many others that season to finish with a record of 22–38, tied for last place with the Boston Celtics in the league's Eastern Division. Troubled by money problems and dwindling attendance, the Huskies folded after that initial season, but the BAA went on for several more years before merging with the National Basketball League (NBL) in 1949 to become the NBA. More than 60 years later, the NBA still regards the Huskies' 68–66 loss to the Knickerbockers as the first game in league history.

COURTSIDE STORIES

TORONTO'S FIRST TEAM

A husky, a stout dog famed for its sled-pulling ability.

itove's first task was to find a leader who would build the Raptors roster, and he chose former Detroit Pistons star Isiah Thomas as vice president of basketball operations. Thomas, in turn, hired former Pistons assistant coach Brendan Malone as the Raptors' head coach. During Thomas and Malone's time together in Detroit, the franchise had won two NBA championships with teams built around the offensive talents of Thomas and a physical brand of defense that stopped other teams cold. In constructing the Raptors, Thomas and Malone hoped to use a similar formula. "We know as an expansion team we may not have a lot of offensive weapons," said Malone. "But we can create offense with tough defense, and we will play tough defense every night."

Toronto's first opportunity to add players to its team came via an expansion draft. Choosing from veterans made available by their former NBA teams, the Raptors would not find any stars, but they did add several solid contributors such as guard Willie Anderson and centers Oliver Miller and Zan Tabak. Then, in the 1995 NBA Draft, the Raptors selected 5-foot-10 point guard Damon Stoudamire from the University of Arizona with the seventh overall pick. Some teams believed that Stoudamire was too small to excel in the NBA, but Thomas, who had been a dominant

player at only 6-foot-1, saw great potential in the young guard. Despite his lack of stature, Stoudamire's speed, passing, and deadly shooting touch allowed him to make a big impact on the game.

On November 3, 1995, the Raptors played their first game, defeating the New Jersey Nets 94–79 at home in Toronto's SkyDome. Even with the promising start, wins would be scarce that first season as the Raptors posted a 21–61 record. Win or lose, Raptors fans were thrilled by the play of Stoudamire, whose steady average of 19 points and 9.3 assists per game earned him the NBA Rookie of the Year award.

Before the 1996–97 season, Thomas made a coaching change, replacing Malone with Darrell Walker. In the Draft, Toronto chose versatile forward Marcus Camby with its first-round pick. The 6-foot-11 Camby gave the Raptors an athletic big man to complement the gifted Stoudamire. Sparked by its two young stars, Toronto's record improved to 30–52, and the future looked bright. "We're young and we're still learning," said Raptors guard Doug Christie. "But we're getting better, and pretty soon, maybe we'll be giving the lessons."

Before joining the new Raptors, guard Willie Anderson spent 7 years with the San Antonio Spurs, scoring 18.6 points per game as a rookie.

DAMON STOUDAMIRE

AT 5-FOOT-10 AND 171 POUNDS, DAMON STOUDAMIRE DID NOT FIT THE USUAL DESCRIPTION OF A FRANCHISE PLAYER IN THE NBA. In a league dominated by giants, the comparatively diminutive Stoudamire proved that a smaller player could not only contribute but could actually excel. Stoudamire had heard the criticism about his size his entire life, but after enjoying a stellar college career at the University of Arizona, he was no longer worried about what others said. In fact, as a child, Stoudamire's favorite cartoon character was Mighty Mouse, who, despite being small, was famous for saving the day. "Mighty Mouse" eventually became Stoudamire's nickname, and after the expansion Toronto Raptors made him their very first draft pick, he quickly became the team's hero. During his rookie season, Stoudamire used his blazing speed and deadly shooting touch to average 19 points and 9.3 assists per game—good enough to earn the 1996 Rookie of the Year award. Throughout his career in Toronto, Stoudamire remained the focal point of the team and the face of the new franchise.

CHAPTER TWO

RAPTORS RELATIVES BRING SUCCESS

Prior to the 1997–98 season, Toronto continued to add young talent through the NBA Draft, using its first-round pick on 18-year-old swingman Tracy McGrady from Mount Zion Christian Academy in North Carolina. Although he came to the league directly from high school, McGrady's physical gifts were impossible to ignore. At 6-foot-8, he boasted a 44-inch vertical leap and was a superb ball handler. "He'll need to develop his shot and grow some man muscles to compete against the kind of athlete he's going to see in the NBA," said Chicago Bulls coach Phil Jackson. "But there is no doubt, if he puts in the work, he'll be a star in this league."

Unfortunately for McGrady and the Raptors, 1997–98 proved to be a disaster. Early on, injuries to key players such as Camby and forwards Walt Williams and Carlos Rogers led to a 17-game losing streak that effectively ended the season

The Raptors took a gamble and got a bargain in the 1997 NBA Draft, obtaining future star Tracy McGrady with the 16th overall selection.

1997 NBA DRAFT

AT&T IBM Sch

	8		A. FOYLE	15			22
RN	9		T. McGRADY	16	CAVS		23
	10	BUCKS		17	MAGIC		24
	11	KINGS		18	BLAZERS		25
	12	Pacers		19	PISTONS		26
	13	CAVS		20			27
	14	CLIPPERS		21			2

NBA DRAFT CHARLOTTE

NBA

WHAT THE TORONTO RAPTORS' FIRST HOME LACKED IN STYLE, IT MADE UP FOR IN SEATING. When the Raptors began play in 1995, they held their home games at SkyDome (now known as the Rogers Centre). The enormous domed stadium provided a spacious setting for the Raptors, with seating for 28,708 fans. Unfortunately, because the stadium was designed for baseball and football, the sight lines for basketball were poor, and the fans' cheers seemed to evaporate inside the cavernous facility. In 1999, the Raptors finally moved into a proper new home, the Air Canada Centre. Named after its airline sponsor, the arena was a major upgrade over SkyDome. Its 19,800 seats, state-of-the-art scoreboard, and fan-friendly facilities brought the game closer to the fans and allowed the Raptors to enjoy a definite home-court advantage. "We packed a lot of people in at SkyDome, but we never heard them," noted forward Vince Carter. "Now, at Air Canada, we know our fans are behind us." Nicknamed "The Hangar," the Air Canada Centre has provided a home to some of the NBA's greatest and most frequent fliers.

before it began. Adding further turmoil, an ownership change during the middle of the season alienated Thomas. Upset that he was not given a larger ownership share and disappointed with the team's performance, Thomas resigned.

After Thomas's departure, the Raptors decided to move away from his philosophy of building with youth. Toronto traded Stoudamire, Williams, and Rogers to the Portland Trail Blazers for guard Alvin Williams, two other players, and three future draft picks. The team also replaced Coach Walker with Butch Carter. The changes did not lead to victories, though, and the Raptors finished the season with a dismal 16–66 record. That summer, Camby was traded to the New York Knicks for veteran forward Charles Oakley.

oing into the 1998–99 season, the Raptors were looking for a player who could energize the franchise. With its first-round pick in the 1998 NBA Draft, Toronto chose forward Antawn Jamison, then traded him to the Golden State Warriors for the rights to rookie forward/ guard Vince Carter. The 6-foot-7 Carter was a great fit for the struggling Raptors. His explosive first step, incredible leaping ability, and knack for producing jaw-dropping highlights promised to bring new excitement and energy to a team that sorely needed it. Toronto fans were excited to see how Carter and McGrady, who were distant cousins, would do on the floor together. Their debut was delayed by a four-month labor dispute between NBA owners and players that shortened the season to 50 games, but once play began in February, the young duo led the Raptors to a respectable 23–27 mark. Carter's averages of 18.3 points and 5.7 rebounds per game opened eyes around the league and earned him the Rookie of the Year award. The season also marked the Raptors' move to their new home—the beautiful Air Canada Centre.

VINCE GOES FOR 51

Vince Carter swoops in for a reverse layup.

VINCE CARTER DID MANY AMAZING THINGS DURING HIS TIME IN TORONTO. The gravity-defying forward/guard was a highlight machine, and fans around the league came out in droves to see what he would do next. On February 27, 2000, Carter put on a show in the Air Canada Centre that would find its way into the record books. That night, Carter and the Raptors hosted the Phoenix Suns. Using an eye-popping variety of moves, including dunks, turnaround jumpers, and long-range bombs from behind the three-point line, Carter exploded for a Raptors-record 51 points in Toronto's 103–102 victory over the Suns. For the game, Carter was 17 of 32 from the field, including 4 of 8 from three-point range, but perhaps his most impressive feat of the night was the least spectacular—he was 13 of 13 from the free-throw line, with several coming near the game's end to clinch the victory for Toronto. "Vince was incredible," said Raptors guard Dee Brown. "He made so many tough shots against a good team in pressure situations—he just willed us to a win."

ncouraged by the team's improvement, Raptors management decided to add some veteran leadership to
assist their developing stars. Prior to the 1999–00

season, the team traded that year's first-round draft pick,

forward Jonathan Bender, to the Indiana Pacers for for-

ward Antonio Davis. The 6-foot-9 and 220-pound Davis

matched with powerful frontcourt mates Oakley and center

Kevin Willis to give Toronto the defense, rebounding, and

strength it had lacked in the past. With the addition of

other veterans such as sharpshooting guard Dell Curry, the

Raptors took another step forward in 1999–00. Led by

Carter and McGrady's combined 41.1 points per game and

Davis and Oakley's combined 15.6 rebounds, the Raptors

soared to the first winning campaign in team history, post-

ing a 45–37 record and clinching their first playoff berth.

COURTSIDE STORIES

PLAYOFFS
AT LAST

Antonio Davis defends the rim
during the 2000 playoffs.

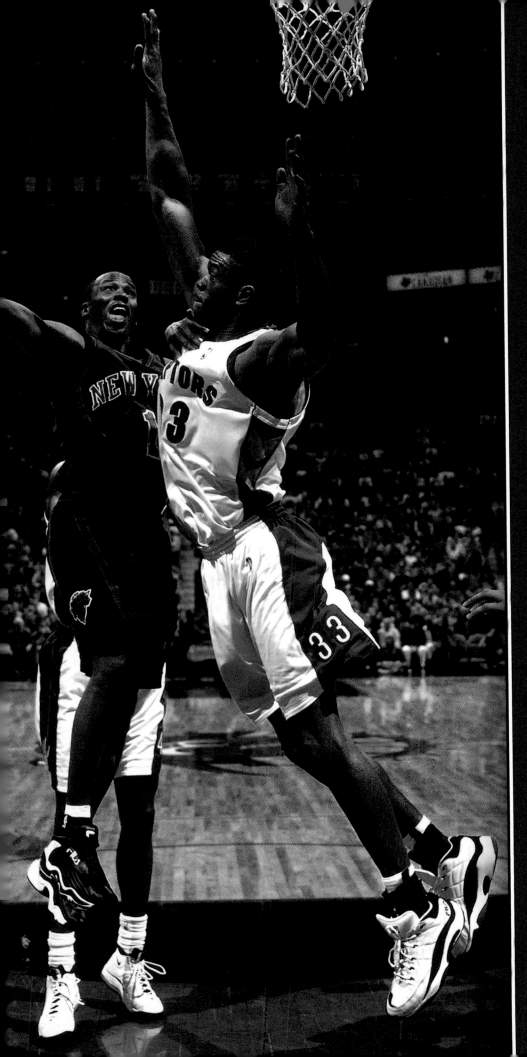

LIKE MOST EXPANSION TEAMS, THE TORONTO RAPTORS SUFFERED THROUGH THEIR SHARE OF LOSING SEASONS DURING THE EARLY YEARS. In its first four seasons, Toronto never posted a winning record and never made the playoffs. But during the 1999–00 season, the Raptors finally broke through. Combining the athleticism of young star swingmen Vince Carter and Tracy McGrady with the veteran muscle of forwards Charles Oakley and Antonio Davis, the Raptors finally posted a winning record of 45–37 and secured a spot in the playoffs. "We really owed this to the people of Toronto for sticking with us during the tough years," said head coach Butch Carter after the team clinched its first trip to the postseason. "We hope we made 'em proud." After losing the first two playoff contests on the road against New York, Toronto hoped that its fired-up home crowd would spur the team to victory, but it was not to be. The Raptors lost 87–80 and were eliminated. Despite the defeat, the 1999–00 Raptors proved one thing—a winner could be built in Toronto.

SOME PLAYERS ARE STARS BECAUSE THEY DO ONE THING EXCEPTIONALLY WELL, BUT DOUG CHRISTIE WAS A STAR BECAUSE HE DID EVERYTHING WELL. A natural athlete, Christie came out of Pepperdine University in 1992 with a reputation as a standout defender. During his early days with the Los Angeles Lakers and New York Knicks, his long arms, quick feet, and aggressive attitude enabled him to consistently shut down opposing teams' best scorers. After moving on to Toronto, Christie continued to dominate defensively for the next five seasons, finishing among the top five in the league in steals three times. In addition to being a shutdown defender for the Raptors, Christie grew to become a steady scorer, deadly three-point shooter, and dependable ball handler. On top of all his physical contributions, Christie was a great leader whose strong work ethic and winning attitude helped transform the young Raptors from a scuffling expansion franchise into a solid playoff contender. "Every team needs its rock, and Doug is ours," said Raptors coach Lenny Wilkens. "Whatever we need, he finds a way to get it done."

INTRODUCING...

DOUG CHRISTIE

POSITION GUARD
HEIGHT 6-FOOT-6
RAPTORS SEASONS 1995–2000

In the first round of postseason play, Toronto drew the powerful Knicks. Each game in the best-of-five series proved to be a close defensive struggle, with no contest decided by more than seven points. But the deeper, more experienced Knicks swept the Raptors in three straight games. "It's a tough blow to take after the season we had," said Carter. "We've got nothing to be ashamed of, though. We gave it all we had."

MOST TEENAGE BOYS ONLY DREAM OF SUCCESS-
FULLY COMPETING AGAINST NBA GREATS, BUT
WHEN TRACY "T-MAC" McGRADY WAS CHOSEN
BY TORONTO WITH THE NINTH OVERALL PICK IN
THE 1997 NBA DRAFT, IT WAS APPARENT THAT HE
WAS NOT GOING TO BE THE AVERAGE TEENAGER.
Despite being only one month past his 18th birthday,
McGrady possessed skills that were advanced beyond

his years. His long body, excellent ball-handling skills,
and explosive speed and leaping ability convinced
scouts he would be a future star. While McGrady's
skills and athleticism were NBA-ready right away, his
strength and maturity needed time to develop. The
Raptors used him carefully during his first two seasons,
allowing him to become accustomed to the league's
speed and physical play, but by his third season,

McGrady began to flash his superstar potential. Team-
ing up with his distant cousin Vince Carter, McGrady
helped lead the Raptors to the franchise's first postseason appearance in 2000. "Watching T-Mac is like
watching a young musical prodigy," said teammate Dell
Curry. "He does things naturally that the rest of us can
only dream about."

CHAPTER THREE

WILKENS TAKES THE REINS

After the encouraging 1999–00 season, the Raptors' hopes for continued improvement were dealt a blow when McGrady was shipped to the Orlando Magic for a first-round draft pick. As McGrady's skills had developed, it had become apparent that his natural position was shooting guard, the same as Carter. Finding it increasingly difficult to play in Carter's growing shadow, McGrady had requested that he be traded, and fearing that he would leave via free agency, the team obliged. The Raptors also made a coaching change, bringing in Lenny Wilkens to replace Butch Carter. Wilkens, one of only three people to be named to the Basketball Hall of Fame as both a player and a coach, had a coaching resumé that included an NBA title with the Seattle Super-Sonics in 1979 and more than 1,000 career victories. The Raptors brought the veteran coach aboard to push the rising team to the next level. "Lenny is a championship-caliber coach, and we think we are ready to contend," said Toronto guard Alvin Williams.

Lenny Wilkens brought a wealth of NBA experience to Toronto in 2000, having played for four different franchises and coached for four.

VINCE CARTER

THERE HAVE BEEN MANY HIGHFLY-ING STARS IN THE HISTORY OF THE NBA, BUT FEW FLEW AS HIGH AS VINCE CARTER. The man nicknamed "Air Canada" and "Half-Man/Half-Amazing" brought energy and excitement to the young Toronto franchise with his mind-boggling dunks and scoring binges. After winning the Rookie of the Year award in 1999, Carter opened even more eyes when he won the NBA Slam Dunk Contest during the 2000 All-Star Game weekend festivities. Capable of incredible aerial acrobatics, Carter seemed to defy gravity when he launched himself toward the basket. His thunderous dunks filled highlight films, and his ability to take over a game offensively was reminiscent of another former University of North Carolina great, Michael Jordan. A five-time All-Star while in Toronto, Carter helped transform the young franchise into a perennial playoff contender. The excitement created by Carter's play even earned its own nickname—"Vinsanity." In Carter's career with Toronto, he scored 40 or more points in a game 12 times and broke the 50-point barrier once. By 2010, he remained the franchise's second all-time leading scorer.

CHAPTER FOUR

TOUGH TIMES IN TORONTO

Prior to the 2003–04 season, Toronto's general manager, Glen Grunwald, promised changes if the Raptors didn't show improvement. After an 8–8 start, Grunwald pulled the trigger on a trade that sent Antonio Davis and forwards Jerome Williams and Chris Jefferies to the Chicago Bulls for guard Jalen Rose and forwards Donyell Marshall and Lonny Baxter. Management hoped that the addition of Rose's ball handling and Marshall's solid scoring would boost an offense that had grown stagnant. "We have to find scoring from people other than Vince Carter," said O'Neill. "The team needs more balance, and Vince needs more help."

By trading Davis, the Raptors were also able to provide more playing time for the team's first-round pick from the 2003 NBA Draft, forward Chris Bosh. Drafted after only one year at the Georgia Institute of Technology (Georgia Tech), the 6-foot-10 and 230-pound Bosh needed playing time to

Jalen Rose was renowned for his versatility; pairing a guard's skills with a 6-foot-8 frame, he could rebound as well as run the point.

develop his considerable skills and gain the strength needed to battle the league's big men. While Bosh performed admirably as a rookie, averaging 11.5 points and 7.4 boards per game, the Raptors fell apart after the All-Star break, posting an 8–24 record down the stretch to finish 33–49. O'Neill was then fired, and Sam Mitchell, a former assistant with the Milwaukee Bucks, was brought in to coach the team.

Before play began for the 2004–05 season, the Eastern Conference was realigned, moving the Raptors to the Atlantic Division. The change did little to help the team's fortunes, however, as Toronto got off to another slow start. Frustrated by the losing, Carter asked to be traded. The struggling Raptors decided to begin rebuilding by trading their marquee star to the New Jersey Nets for center Alonzo Mourning, forwards Eric Williams and Aaron Williams, and two first-round draft picks. The deal took a bad turn for Toronto when Mourning, a seven-time All-Star, refused to report to the team. The Raptors were eventually forced to sell his contract to the Miami Heat, and without the veteran pivotman, the young, undersized Raptors struggled again. Despite the contributions of

Forward Eric Williams got used to many uniforms, suiting up for six different NBA teams in the four seasons from 2003–04 to 2006–07.

SAM MITCHELL KNEW WHAT IT TOOK TO TURN AROUND A STRUGGLING EXPANSION FRANCHISE. As one of the original players for the expansion Minnesota Timberwolves from 1989 to 1992 and again from 1995 to 2002, he learned the lesson that losing can be a hard habit to break if you give in to it. The tenacious Mitchell never gave in, and by the time his playing career ended in 2002, Minnesota was a consistent winner. When Mitchell became head coach of the Raptors, the franchise was suffering through a stretch of losing seasons. Few gave the first-time coach much of a chance to turn the team around, but Mitchell had faith. As a coach, his bullish, defensive-minded, and aggressive style was reflective of the way he had played. Slowly but surely, Mitchell transformed Toronto from a lifeless loser into one of the league's hardest-working teams. By his third season, Mitchell had led the Raptors to their first division title. "Winning is paid for with talent and effort," said Mitchell. "Talent is great, but if you don't play with heart, you aren't going anywhere."

INTRODUCING...

SAM MITCHELL

COACH
RAPTORS SEASONS 2004–08

guard Rafer Alston, Rose, and Bosh, the Raptors finished 33–49 for the second straight season.

Toronto's troubles continued in 2005–06. Mitchell consistently got strong efforts out of players such as guard Mike James and rookie forward Charlie Villanueva, but the team's thin bench and inexperience doomed the Raptors to a 27–55 record. One bright spot during the down year was the play of Bosh. In his third year, the once-skinny 21-year-old had added 15 more pounds of muscle to his long frame. Bosh averaged 22.5 points and 9.2 rebounds per game, good enough to earn a spot on his first All-Star team. "When Chris first got here, he was a kid, but we needed him to play like a man," said Toronto guard Morris Peterson. "Now Chris is a man. He's worked hard to develop his game, and this is his team now."

CHAPTER FIVE

BACK ON TRACK

The Raptors' run of bad luck seemed to change at last when the team won the NBA Draft lottery, giving it the top overall pick in the 2006 Draft. With it, the team chose forward Andrea Bargnani from Italy. The 20-year-old Bargnani was the first European player ever selected with the number-one pick. The Raptors believed his size (seven feet), agility, and ability to shoot from all over the floor would make him an impact player. In another move, Toronto traded Villanueva to the Milwaukee Bucks for speedy point guard T. J. Ford. The Raptors loved Ford's ability to push the basketball, penetrate defenses, and either score or create an easy basket for a teammate. Toronto also added free agent guard Anthony Parker, who had spent several seasons playing overseas and developed into a solid three-point shooter and tenacious defender.

Known in his native Italy as "The Magician," Andrea Bargnani gave Toronto a refined shooting touch and steadily improving defense.

The Raptors' remake was engineered by new general manager Bryan Colangelo, son of longtime Phoenix Suns owner Jerry Colangelo. The younger Colangelo realized that basketball was now a worldwide game and that great talent could be found in many countries. His plan to rebuild the Raptors focused on global scouting for the best talent available, regardless of what country the player was from. "The days of the world's best basketball players coming only from the United States are long over," said Colangelo. "Toronto is an international city, and I guess it makes sense the Raptors should be an international team."

Thanks to Colangelo's moves, Toronto fans saw immediate improvement during the 2006–07 season. Bosh again led the way, averaging 22.6 points and 10.7 rebounds per game, but this time he had help from Bargnani, Ford, and Parker, all of whom averaged more than 11 points a game. The Raptors soared to a 47–35 mark and captured their first Atlantic Division title. Ironically, in the playoffs, Toronto's opponent was the Vince Carter-led New Jersey Nets. The upstart Raptors gave the veteran Nets a tough fight, but they eventually lost the series, four games to two.

Hopes were high for Toronto in 2007–08, but injuries to Ford and Bosh limited the team's effectiveness. One bright spot was the play of

guard Jose Calderon. A native of Spain, Calderon averaged 11.2 points and 8.3 assists per game and proved to be a quality starter while Ford was out. Despite Calderon's emergence, the Raptors slipped to a 41–41 record and were eliminated by the Orlando Magic in five games in the first round of the playoffs.

Prior to the 2008–09 season, Colangelo revised the roster again, this time trading Ford, center Rasho Nesterovic, forward Maceo Baston, and a first-round draft pick to the Indiana Pacers for power forward Jermaine O'Neal. The Raptors hoped the six-time All-Star would make the team a title contender, but unfortunately, the experiment did not work out. After an 8–9 start, Toronto quickly slid to the bottom of the division, finishing with a 33–49 record. As Toronto's lineup continue to change, the Raptors—behind Bosh, Bargnani, Calderon, and guard Jarrett Jack—improved to 40–42 in 2009–10 but missed the playoffs yet again.

ONE OF THE NBA'S BEST YOUNG PLAYERS OF THE 2000s, TEXAS NATIVE CHRIS BOSH QUICKLY BECAME THE HEART AND SOUL OF THE TORONTO RAPTORS. Only 19 years old when he was taken fourth overall in the 2003 NBA Draft, Bosh willingly—and admirably—battled NBA veterans 10 years older and 30 pounds heavier his rookie year, earning their respect. At 6-foot-10 and with a 7-foot-3 wingspan, Bosh's incredibly long body soon made him an excellent shot blocker and ferocious finisher around the basket. Graceful and fast for a big man, Bosh ran the floor with abandon, often punctuating fast breaks with powerful dunks. His range beyond the three-point line, fun-loving personality, and numerous charitable works also endeared the man known as "CB4" (in reference to his initials and jersey number) to players and fans alike. "Chris Bosh is an incredible young man," said Raptors coach Sam Mitchell. "He gives you everything he's got on the court, he inspires his teammates, and he gives back to the community. It's rare to see that kind of maturity in someone so young."

PRIOR TO THE 2008–09 SEASON, TORONTO FANS DIDN'T HAVE TO WORRY ABOUT TWO OF THEIR STAR PLAYERS STAYING IN SHAPE. Chris Bosh and Jose Calderon were busy competing in the 2008 Summer Olympics, held in Beijing, China. Calderon played for his home country of Spain, while Bosh represented the U.S. During the Games, Calderon's Spanish team won four of its five matchups in pool play to advance to the Medal Tournament, while Bosh and Team USA advanced with a 5–0 record. In the tournament, both teams dominated the opposition, setting up a Spain versus USA showdown for the gold medal. In the game, Team USA fought off a strong effort from the Spaniards to claim a hard-fought 118–107 victory. "Winning the gold medal for my country is something I will remember forever," said Bosh. Calderon, who had to miss the gold medal game because of injury, had similar feelings. "It is an honor to play for my country," said the Spanish star. "I just wish I could have had the chance to play against Chris for the gold medal."

BOSH AND CALDERON VIE FOR GOLD

Spaniard Jose Calderon in action during the 2008 Olympics.

The city of Toronto is a gathering place for people from all over the world, famous for its welcoming ways and willingness to embrace new and different things. More than a decade has passed since the NBA took a chance on a Canadian city that many experts thought would never grow to love the sport of basketball. Toronto has proven that basketball could not only survive in Canada—it could thrive. Through good times and bad, Toronto fans have backed their Raptors with boundless hope and enthusiasm. Those fans await the day when this city of open arms will at last be able to embrace an NBA championship.

Turkish forward Hedo Turkoglu brought sharpshooting—and yet another nationality—to the Raptors lineup when he arrived in 2009.

INDEX

A
Air Canada Centre 18, 20, 21
All-Star Game 33, 39
Alston, Rafer 39
Anderson, Willie 11
B
BAA-NBL merger 10
Bargnani, Andrea 40, 42, 43
Basketball Hall of Fame 28
Baston, Maceo 43
Baxter, Lonny 35
Bitove, John Jr. 8, 11
Bosh, Chris 35, 36, 39, 42, 43, 44–45, 46
Brown, Dee 21
C
Calderon, Jose 43, 46
Camby, Marcus 13, 16, 19
Carter, Butch 19, 23, 28
Carter, Vince 18, 20, 21, 22, 23, 25, 27, 28, 30, 31, 32–33, 35, 36, 42
Christie, Doug 13, 24
Colangelo, Bryan 42
Curry, Dell 22, 27
D
Davis, Antonio 22, 23, 30, 35
division championships 38, 42
F
Ford, T. J. 40, 42, 43
G
Grunwald, Glen 35
J
Jack, Jarrett 43
James, Mike 39
Jefferies, Chris 35
L
Lenard, Voshon 31
M
Malone, Brendan 11, 13
Marshall, Donyell 35
McGrady, Tracy 16, 20, 22, 23, 26–27, 28
Miller, Oliver 11
Mitchell, Sam 36, 38, 39, 45

N
Naismith, James 9
Nesterovic, Rasho 43
O
Oakley, Charles 19, 22, 23
Olajuwon, Hakeem 30–31
O'Neal, Jermaine 43
O'Neill, Kevin 31, 35, 36
P
Parker, Anthony 40, 42
Peterson, Morris 30, 31, 39
playoffs 22, 23, 24, 25, 27, 30, 31, 33, 42, 43
R
Rogers, Carlos 16, 19
Rookie of the Year award 13, 15, 20, 33
Rose, Jalen 35, 39
S
SkyDome 13, 18
Slam Dunk Contest 33
Stoudamire, Damon 11, 13, 14–15, 19
T
Tabak, Zan 11
team name 8
team records 21, 33
Thomas, Isiah 11, 13, 19
Toronto Huskies 10
V
Villanueva, Charlie 39, 40
W
Walker, Darrell 13, 19
Wilkens, Lenny 24, 28, 30, 31
Williams, Aaron 36
Williams, Alvin 19, 28
Williams, Eric 36
Williams, Jerome 35
Williams, Walt 16, 19
Willis, Kevin 22